# NATURE'S MYSTERIES

# WHIRLPOOLS

**SARA HOWELL**

Britannica
Educational Publishing

IN ASSOCIATION WITH

ROSEN
EDUCATIONAL SERVICES

PLAINV

Plainv

MAY – – 2017

Published in 2017 by Britannica Educational Publishing (a trademark of Encyclopædia Britannica, Inc.) in association with The Rosen Publishing Group, Inc.
29 East 21st Street, New York, NY 10010

Distributed exclusively by Rosen Publishing.
To see additional Britannica Educational Publishing titles, go to rosenpublishing.com.

First Edition

**Britannica Educational Publishing**
J.E. Luebering: Executive Director, Core Editorial
Mary Rose McCudden: Editor, Britannica Student Encyclopedia

**Rosen Publishing**
Shalini Saxena: Editor
Nelson Sá: Art Director
Michael Moy: Designer
Cindy Reiman: Photography Manager
Karen Huang: Photo Researcher

**Library of Congress Cataloging-in-Publication Data**

Names: Howell, Sara, author.
Title: Whirlpools / Sara Howell.
Description: First edition. | New York : Britannica Educational Publishing,
  in association with the Rosen Publishing Group, Inc., 2017. | 2017 |
  Series: Nature's mysteries | Audience: Grades 1 to 4._ | Includes
  bibliographical references and index.
Identifiers: LCCN 2015047014| ISBN 9781680484854 (library bound : alk. paper)
  | ISBN 9781680484939 (pbk. : alk. paper) | ISBN 9781680484625 (6-pack :
  alk. paper)
Subjects: LCSH: Whirlpools—Juvenile literature. | Vortex-motion—Juvenile
  literature. | Water currents—Juvenile literature.
Classification: LCC GC239 .H69 2017 | DDC 551.46—dc23
LC record available at http://lccn.loc.gov/2015047014

*Manufactured in the United States of America*

**Photo credits:** Cover, pp. 1, 4 Nicolas Le Corre/Gamma-Rapho/Getty Images; cover, p. 1 (cloudburst graphic) Macrovector/Shutterstock.com; p. 5 Comstock/Thinkstock; p. 6 Richard Eskite Photography/Photolibrary/Getty Images; p. 7 Alan Copson/AWL Images/Getty Images; p. 8 NASA; pp. 9, 12, 26 Encyclopædia Britannica, Inc.; p. 10 © Merriam-Webster Inc.; pp. 11, 22 © Zoonar GmbH/Alamy Stock Photo; p. 13 Matt Cardy/Getty Images; p. 14 Rich Reid/National Geographic Image Collection/Getty Images; p. 15 U.S. Geological Survey; p. 16 Michael S. Yamashita/National Geographic Magazines/Getty Images; pp. 17, 29 Kyodo/AP Images; p. 18 © Danita Delimont/Alamy Stock Photo; p. 19 Steve Fleming/Moment/Getty Images; p. 20 Nomad/SuperStock; p. 21 © Prisma Bildagentur AG/Alamy Stock Photo; p. 23 © Scottish Viewpoint/Alamy Stock Photo; p. 24 © bilwissedition Ltd. & Co. KG/Alamy Stock Photo; p. 25 © amana images inc./Alamy Stock Photo; p. 27 Bernhard Staehli/Shutterstock.com; p. 28 © iStockphoto.com/slava296 interior pages background patterns Eky Studio/Shutterstock.com (rays), zffoto/Shutterstock.com (waves); back cover, interior pages background image helloseed/Shutterstock.com.

# CONTENTS

# A SWIRLING MYSTERY

The world around us contains many amazing and mysterious features. One such phenomenon is called a whirlpool. Whirlpools are water that moves very quickly in a circle. They can be found anywhere in Earth's oceans, rivers, and lakes. They can be any size. Tiny whirlpools can be found in your home when water drains from your sink or bathtub.

Hundreds of years ago, sailors wondered if whirlpools could be giant undersea monsters or gates to another world. Today we know that

**Several different forces can cause water to swirl and form a whirlpool.**

**VOCABULARY**

A **tsunami** is a very high, large wave in the ocean that is usually caused by an earthquake under the sea and that can cause great destruction when it reaches land.

whirlpools are not as mysterious as they seem and that they can be explained with science. A combination of natural forces that exist in our world can cause whirlpools to form.

Situations created by nature or accidentally by humans may set off forces that result in whirlpools. These situations can include ocean tides, sinkholes, or **tsunamis**. Though scientists can now explain what whirlpools are and why they exist, scientists continue to wonder at how beautiful and violently dangerous they can be.

Some sinkholes, such as the one seen here, occur naturally. Others are the result of human actions.

# VISUALIZING A VORTEX

If you fill a bathtub or sink with water and then pull the drain, a whirlpool will form as water goes down the drain. The water will swirl in a circular motion. The diameter, or measurement across the center of the circle, is wider at the top and narrows as the water moves down. The funnel-shaped swirling mass of water, called a vortex, will pull any floating objects around it into its center. A vortex can also be

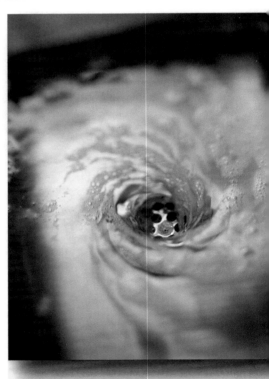

Water swirling down a drain can move in either a clockwise or counterclockwise direction.

the swirling mass of air in a tornado. This is why a whirlpool looks very much like a tornado.

Whirlpools can form in many different sizes. Some may have a diameter of only a few inches. Others can be more than 30 feet (9 meters) across. One of the largest known whirlpools measures more than 250 feet (76 meters) in diameter. That is about as long as a soccer field. In large whirlpools, the water can rush through the vortex at great speeds. The rushing water can make loud roaring noises that can be heard from far away.

**Here a whirlpool occurs off the coast of the Canary Islands in the Atlantic Ocean.**

# OCEANS ALL AROUND

**Although we spend most of our time on land, most of Earth's surface is water.**

To understand whirlpools, it is important to understand the environment in which they appear. Whirlpools can occur in any body of water, such as a river or a lake. There are also many opportunities for whirlpools to form in an ocean. An ocean is a huge body of salt water. Oceans cover nearly 71 percent of Earth's surface. They contain almost 98 percent of all the water on Earth.

## THINK ABOUT IT

Oceans contain many great sources of food for people around the world. They also provide minerals, oil, and natural gas. How else are oceans important to life on Earth?

There are four main oceans on Earth: the Pacific, the Atlantic, the Indian, and the Arctic. These oceans have no real borders, and water flows freely between them. Smaller parts of these oceans are called seas, gulfs, and bays.

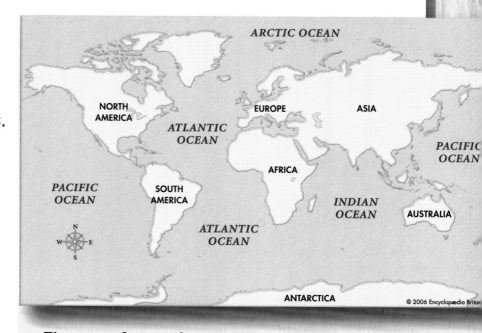

There are four major oceans, but there are also other bodies of water in which whirlpools can form.

# MOVING WATER

**W**hirlpools appear when water moves in certain ways. Winds, tides, and other natural forces cause ocean water to constantly move around Earth in patterns called currents. In different parts of the world, currents move in different directions. For example, the main ocean currents of the half of Earth above the Equator (or the Northern Hemisphere) move in a clockwise direction. Below the Equator,

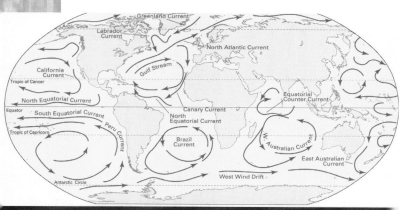

**On this map, you can see the major surface currents of Earth's oceans.**

## COMPARE AND CONTRAST

Ocean currents carry heat and can affect the climate, or the weather in a place over time. How do you think a warm ocean current might affect the weather of nearby land differently than a cold ocean current?

in the southern half of Earth (or the Southern Hemisphere) ocean currents move in a counterclockwise direction. At the Equator, the currents move from east to west.

Whirlpools often occur when two currents moving in opposite directions meet. If the two currents are powerful enough, they may wrap around each other. This movement creates a circular current, or an eddy. Circular currents or eddies are other names for whirlpools.

This whirlpool is located in Saltstraumen, a narrow water passage in Norway. It has the strongest tidal current in the world.

# CHANGING TIDES

A long the coasts of every ocean on Earth, the water level changes on a regular basis. This movement is known as the tide. Ocean tides affect currents and can create whirlpools.

Tides are caused by a natural force called gravity. All bodies in the universe pull on each other because of gravity. The Sun and the Moon both pull on Earth, but

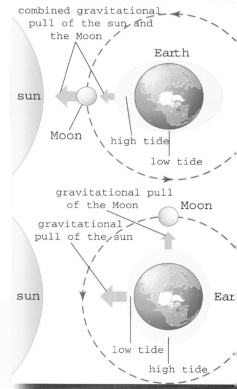

**This diagram shows how the position of the Sun, Moon, and Earth can affect the movement of Earth's water.**

# THINK ABOUT IT

**Because of gravity, the Sun and the Moon both pull on Earth. Why would the pull of the Moon have a greater influence?**

the Moon has a greater effect on Earth's tides than the Sun. As the Moon pulls on Earth, it makes the water move. On the side of Earth near the Moon, the water builds up in a wave. Another wave forms on the other side of Earth. These waves result in high tide. The water on the sides of Earth that are not being pulled by the Moon is at low tide. As Earth rotates, or spins, and the Moon moves around Earth, the tides change. Because the Moon moves around Earth in a regular path, the cycle of the tides follows a regular pattern.

**There are two high and two low tides each day at any given place, but the times of the tides change every day.**

# IDEAL CONDITIONS

Tides take place in all bodies of water. In some waters, however, the change is so small that it may be difficult to notice. Tides are easier to see where an ocean meets land. As the water levels rise and fall, they create motion across the water, which causes tidal currents. The tidal currents create conditions that can cause a whirlpool to form.

Whirlpools may form when water moves rapidly through a narrow channel

**Queen Charlotte Strait runs through part of British Columbia, in Canada.**

called a **strait**. Straits connect two larger bodies of water. They are often shallower than the larger bodies of water that they connect. If the strait has an irregular shape, it may cause the water that moves rapidly through it to form a whirlpool. Physical features of the ocean floor, such as peaks and trenches, can also affect the movement of the water.

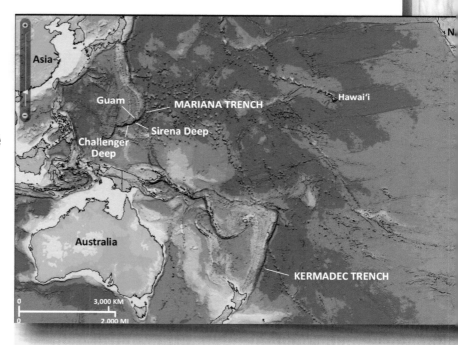

The Mariana Trench, shown here, is the deepest point on Earth.

# TSUNAMIS AND EARTHQUAKES

Because tides and currents follow regular patterns, some whirlpools around the world appear in roughly the same place each day. In some cases, though, whirlpools can be caused by sudden events. These whirlpools may last for a few minutes or a few hours and then disappear.

In March 2011 a powerful earthquake struck beneath the Pacific Ocean. The earthquake triggered a huge tsunami that hit the country of Japan and caused major damage. The tsunami also created a massive whirlpool off the country's coast.

**Tsunami waves triggered by an undersea earthquake caused massive destruction in Japan in 2011.**

In 1812 a series of earthquakes called the New Madrid earthquakes struck near Missouri. The earthquakes caused the water in parts of the Mississippi River to flow in the opposite direction and to rise and fall rapidly. Much of the land in the area was destroyed, and whirlpools and other water features, such as waterfalls, appeared suddenly on the Mississippi.

The photo on the left shows the whirlpool created by the 2011 tsunami. The same area is shown a year later, on the right.

# WATER FROM ABOVE

Another place that a whirl-pool can form is at the base of a waterfall. A waterfall is a place in a river where water spills suddenly downward. The action of flowing river water causes **weathering** to take place. It is one of the most

The whirlpool at the base of Starvation Creek Falls, in Oregon, can be seen by the movement of maple leaves on the surface of the water.

common causes of waterfalls. The flowing water wears away soft rock. The hard rock that remains creates a steep wall, which the river water plunges over to form a waterfall. Waterfalls may also form as a result of movements in Earth's crust.

The rapid flow of water in a waterfall can be very powerful. As the water crashes to the bottom, it can create whirlpools. These whirlpools erode more rock beneath them.

This canyon in Iceland gets 10 inches (25 centimeters) longer yearly because of erosion caused by the water.

# HUMAN-MADE WHIRLPOOLS

The fact that a whirlpool can form naturally is fascinating. It is equally fascinating, however, that whirlpools can be created by the actions of humans! Mining and drilling for Earth's natural resources can lead to conditions that form whirlpools.

In 1980 an oil rig was drilling in Lake Peigneur, in Louisiana. Beneath the lake

**The powerful Lake Peigneur whirlpool sucked trees, barges, and soil from the surrounding area down into the mine below.**

# COMPARE AND CONTRAST

**Compare and contrast the natural and human-made conditions that cause whirlpools to form. How are they similar? How are they different?**

was a large salt mine. A drill on the oil rig broke through the floor of the lake and created a hole leading to the mine below. This caused the lake to behave like a giant bathtub, creating a whirlpool as the water drained into the salt mine.

In June 2015 engineers began draining some of the water from Lake Texoma, between Texas and Oklahoma. They opened the floodgates of a nearby dam. The movement of the water formed a powerful sucking whirlpool with a diameter more than 8 feet (2.4 meters) wide!

**Lake Texoma is a human-made reservoir created by the Denison Dam.**

# FAMOUS WHIRLPOOLS

**M**ost tides and ocean currents flow in regular patterns. Because of this, some whirlpools have been forming in the same spot for hundreds of years!

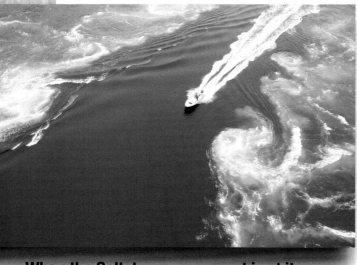

When the Saltstraumen current is at its strongest, water rushes through the strait at about 20 miles (32 kilometers) per hour.

One of the most famous whirlpools is Moskstraumen, off the coast of Norway. It is a large area of strong currents that was described in stories by authors Jules Verne and Edgar Allan Poe. Another name for the area is Maelstrom. The word "maelstrom" is now used as a name for any powerful whirlpool.

Another mighty whirlpool off the coast of Norway is named Saltstraumen. It is considered to have the strongest tidal currents in the world.

One of the world's largest whirlpools is Corryvreckan. It is located off the coast of Scotland. A large whirlpool off the Atlantic Coast of Canada is called the Old Sow. Some say it is named after the grunting noises it makes that sound similar to the sounds that pigs make. It is located in the Bay of Fundy.

**The roar of the Corryvreckan whirlpool can be heard from 10 miles (16 kilometers) away.**

# DANGER IN THE SEA

Whirlpools can be massive, powerful, and loud. A strong enough whirlpool, or vortex, can pull debris into its center. Whirlpools can also appear as crashing swirls of water. For these reasons, many old stories described whirlpools as deadly, violent, or even

This illustration shows a ship passing between Charybdis on the left and Scylla, another mythical monster, on the right.

supernatural. A whirlpool off the coast of Sicily was often considered to be a mythical sea monster named Charybdis.

Despite these stories, though, most whirlpools are not very dangerous. Most are not strong enough to pull in large ships. Ships are also able to avoid areas where whirlpools are known to form. However, swimmers and small boats must always be careful around whirlpools or any strong currents. In 1947 author George Orwell had to be rescued after his boat was nearly pulled into the Corryvreckan whirlpool!

**Modern technology and navigation techniques help ships to avoid large whirlpools.**

# OUR CHANGING CLIMATE

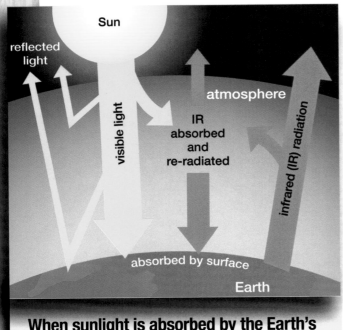

Sun

reflected light

atmosphere

visible light

IR absorbed and re-radiated

infrared (IR) radiation

absorbed by surface

Earth

**When sunlight is absorbed by the Earth's surface and atmosphere, it can lead to global warming.**

Many of today's scientists are increasingly concerned about how Earth's average surface temperature is gradually rising. This trend is known as global warming. Global warming causes Earth's climate to change. Climate change can greatly affect all environments on Earth. This includes the way that ocean currents behave. Any changes to the pattern of

## COMPARE AND CONTRAST

An area's climate determines what kinds of plants and animals can survive there. How could certain environments on Earth change if their average temperatures rose or fell greatly?

how ocean currents behave would also affect where, when, or even if a whirlpool forms.

Climate is the weather found in a certain place over a long period of time. As Earth's overall temperature becomes warmer over time, huge glaciers, or large masses of ice, melt. As they melt, their fresh water enters the salty ocean. This fresh water can change how certain currents flow around the world. Even a small change in ocean currents could affect the Earth's climate in major ways!

Glaciers all around the world are melting, and their rates of melting are speeding up.

# MYSTERY SOLVED

Whirlpools are one of nature's most fascinating displays. Though they may look mysterious, their existence can be explained by science. Most whirlpools are formed by a regular pattern of tides and ocean currents. Others form at the bottoms of waterfalls or after major events in the ocean, such as

Human-made whirlpools, such as this one at a waterpark, are often created with equipment called hydraulic pumps.

## COMPARE AND CONTRAST

Whirlpools are a type of vortex that involves liquid. What are some other vortexes you have seen? How are they similar to and different from a whirlpool?

earthquakes or tsunamis. You might see a human-made whirlpool at a waterpark and have probably noticed one in a sink or bathtub!

Today we know that massive whirlpools are not giant monsters or holes leading to the center of Earth. However, it is not hard to understand why whirlpools inspired such stories, as they are an amazing sight. Each year, people come from all over the world to view the swirling, turbulent waters of the world's most powerful whirlpools.

The Naruto whirlpools in Japan are a popular tourist attraction.

# GLOSSARY

**CLIMATE** The usual weather conditions found in a certain place.

**CLIMATE CHANGE** A change in the usual weather conditions found in certain regions on Earth. Climate change has recently sped up because of human activity. Over time, climate change happens naturally at a slow pace.

**CRUST** The outer, or top, layer of Earth.

**CURRENT** Water or air that continuously flows in one direction.

**DAM** A barrier that blocks the flow of water.

**DEBRIS** The remains of something broken down or destroyed.

**DIAMETER** The distance through the center of a round or circular body.

**EDDY** A current of air or water running against the main current or in a circle; another word for eddy is vortex or whirlpool.

**GLACIERS** Large masses of freshwater ice that slowly flow over land.

**GRAVITY** The natural pulling force that causes objects to move toward each other's centers. Because objects on Earth are much smaller than Earth, their gravity is not as strong as Earth's and they fall toward Earth's center.

**GULFS** Large areas of ocean partly surrounded by land.

**HEMISPHERE** One of the halves of Earth.

**PHENOMENON** Something that can be seen and studied but is difficult to understand or explain.

**SINKHOLES** Low areas or holes in the ground most often formed when soil and rocks are removed by flowing water.

**TRENCHES** Long narrow cracks in the ocean floor.

**VORTEX** A mass of spinning air, liquid, or other substance that pulls things into its center.

## Books

Benoit, Peter. *Climate Change*. New York, NY: Children's Press, 2011.

Koontz, Robin. *The Science of a Tsunami*. North Mankato, MN: Cherry Lake Publishing, 2016.

Macquitty, Miranda. *Ocean*. New York, NY: DK Publishing, 2014.

Olien, Rebecca. *Water Sources* (Water in Our World). North Mankato, MN: Capstone Press, 2016.

Winchester, Simon. *When the Earth Shakes: Earthquakes, Volcanoes, and Tsunamis*. New York, NY: Viking Books for Young Readers, 2015.

## Websites

Because of the changing nature of Internet links, Rosen Publishing has developed an online list of websites related to the subject of this book. This site is updated regularly. Please use this link to access this list:

http://www.rosenlinks.com/NMY/whirl

# INDEX